S0-BYH-529

Offline Journal

un

The Unnamed Press
Los Angeles, CA

AN UNNAMED PRESS BOOK

The Unnamed Press
P.O. Box 411272
Los Angeles, CA 90041

Copyright © 2019 Jaya Nicely

All rights reserved, including the right to reproduce this book or portions
thereof in any form whatsoever. Permissions inquiries may be directed
to info@unnamedpress.com. Published in North America by the Unnamed Press.

www.unnamedpress.com

Unnamed Press, and the colophon, are registered trademarks of Unnamed Media LLC.

Library of Congress Cataloging-in-Publication Data is available.

Designed & typeset by Jaya Nicely.

ISBN 978-1-944700-7-99

Distributed by Publishers Group West
Manufactured in Canada

First Edition

1 3 5 7 9 10 8 6 4 2

Offline Journal

Jaya Nicely

Leave your phone at home...

With the world in our pocket, it's almost impossible to disconnect. Not long ago, I created a project for myself that forced me to step out of my comfort zone, engage with my environment and leave technology behind. I traveled around my city documenting different neighborhoods, the people that lived there and the sights and smells I came across. I discovered so many different things that I would have missed by staying glued to my phone and found inspiration everywhere I went! Instead of online content carefully curated by strangers, I was discovering new things for myself that I loved. Most importantly, I left my phone behind.

Getting out of a rut or pushing yourself creatively means breaking out of a routine and taking risks. And being constantly attached to your phone can be just that: *a rut.*

Sometimes it was scary to go outside and do it by myself. Some days it was hard to find motivation to make something new...or to log out and create instead! I don't want you to feel the same way, so I've designed this workbook to be your companion and guide. These pages will help you pay attention to the little things you can miss every day, push you to think outside of the norm, to try something new and gain a new set of skills in the process. Instead of scrolling down endless feeds, ditch your phone, pick up this book, and fill out a page. By the end you'll wind up with something uniquely and unequivocally *you.* -Jaya

How to use this Book:

Whether you can take a day, a week, or five minutes to be offline, what matters is how you spend that time. Even giving yourself ten minutes a day to connect directly with yourself is worth it. This book helps no matter how much time you have.

1. Turn your phone off, shut your laptop, look around and appreciate that you are here, right now, in the world. How wonderful is that?

2. Offline Journal is organized to help you spend a day offline from morning to night, but no matter what time it is, there are three main opportunities you can take advantage of anytime you aren't looking at a screen:

Connection
(Morning)

Productivity
& Presence
(Afternoon)

Rest & Reflection
(Evening)

Paint or
test out your
materials

Use whatever
tools you feel
comfortable with

Sketch and
document your
surroundings

Write, make lists, or
come up with stories

Plan, map, and organize

3. The creative prompts in this book are intended to inspire you no matter who you are or what you like to do. Remember, this journal is a jumping off point for your life in reality. It's easy to escape and check-out, but the act of unplugging (even for short amounts of time) will lead to deeper connections with yourself and others.

Offline Morning: Connection

"I've always wanted to be able to paint the dawn." - David Hockney

Check yourself:

Do you check Instagram as soon as your alarm goes off? When's the last time you went for a walk and didn't take a picture? For me, the key to a day offline is ditching my phone altogether.

Instead of email or news, I take a personal inventory. What am I feeling? What am I grateful for? What do I really need from today?

morning inventory

Connection: Rediscovering yourself and your environment offline leads to deeper understanding.

Community
Appreciating
where you live

Nature
Recognizing the
planet we all share

Roots
Rediscovering where
you come from

Feelings
Looking inward
in order to grow

Color Theory (for your life):

For a designer or artist, creating a color palette involves choosing a group of colors that complement the mood or tone of their work. When I go offline, I pick a palette of things that are important to me, and I stick with them. What are your priorities right now? What do you want to achieve today? For the next list you make, assign colors to the tasks or ideas.

Sometimes I look at the sky for color inspiration...

Blue skies call for meditation and reflection

enjoy the sunrise on an early morning hike

cold, grey days mean canceled plans and catching up on projects

or I look at what I eat...

Fuji apples for new ideas

Plums for perseverance

Gala apples for high priorities

today's palette:

Pop-hop books

Garvanza Skate Park

I get all my cards, pens, and stationery here.

Shorthand
5030

Pinball, asian fusion food, and great beer—what more could you ask for?

Franny is the guard at Skylight Books...don't pet!

BUTTON MASH

SEYMO

Places to Discover Phone-free.

Sunset NURSERY

I love seeing what new plants they get in every month!

My favorite place to walk is the Huntington Library and Gardens

Liz runs Ginger Corner Market, my favorite sandwich place

The owner of Nature's Perfections is always willing to give advice and a great deal on your plants!

Marcel Proust said, "You don't need an unfamiliar landscape to discover new things, just new eyes." Phone-free, step outside, keep your head up and remember: the real world is actually the one all around you.

What's your Sign?

The moment you step outside your door, you see signs meant to grab attention. But the best signs transport you to a different time or place. They deliver a feeling!

Sunset Blvd.

Eagle Rock Blvd.

Colorado Blvd.

Thank You

Lake Ave.

What signs make you smile?

Finding Patterns: I love to discover nature in its details, which are consistently perfect.

Peacock Plant

Philodendron Brasil

Ficus elastica

Calathea Ornata

Maranta prayer plant

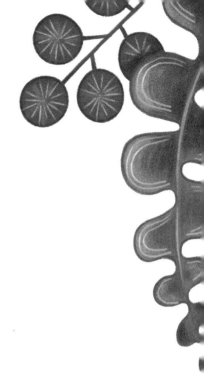

The Dream Plant: Living in the city,
I sometimes struggle to find nature. The Dream Plant grows only in one place: your imagination. What does yours look like? What is the pattern of its leaves? How often does it bloom?

"Nature does not hurry;
yet everything is accomplished."
-Lao Tzu

The next time you sit down at a coffee shop, keep your eyes up. Take a few moments to get your bearings. Then choose an interesting subject. Describe or sketch them. Imagine what is going on in their life.

"we really need to up our social media game, guys."

"I don't even know what cold brew is."

"Has he texted you yet?!"

"yeah, I'm getting, like, really into photography."

Without a phone, I no longer have to make food the star of my Instagram account. I can truly appreciate what I am eating, as well as what's going on (or being said) around me.

What's your route?

Imagining your favorite places together, they become a personal neighborhood, unique to you. Try visiting them without your phone, and discover them with new eyes. You can map them here.

Connect with your Roots:

Use your day offline to reconnect with real things... I like to take a trip up the coast to visit my grandma and go back to old comforts.

the curlers she wears to bed

homemade apple pie

vintage books

old butter tubs used as tupperware

List some everyday objects in your home that have a deeper meaning to you. Write about a specific memory they bring up.

I'll sit with my grandmother looking out the kitchen window at all the birds that visit her feeders. Now, no matter where I am, I look for the birds that live there.

Thich Nhat Hanh says that, "We have to remember that our body is not limited to what lies within the boundary of our skin. Our body is much more immense." We rely on so many physical things throughout our day, but what are some vital feelings that keep us truly alive?

What's vital to you?

Offline, you can be truly present for the little moments that fill you with joy.

Opening a brand new journal

squishing a cat paw

Staying in bed on a rainy day

When the waiter
brings your food

Walking
through crunchy
Fall leaves

Receiving
a bouquet

Offline Afternoon: Productivity & Presence

"Making a whole is very important. Most people paint things and forget the whole."
-Tove Jansson

Discover Yourself: Time to center yourself and stay organized.

How does it feel to be unplugged? Is it uncomfortable to not be able to check messages? Are you anxious about what you have missed? Or are you beginning to let go?

afternoon inventory

Awareness: To be truly productive and present, you have to be aware of what is happening around you.

Space

Space is important,
it's what holds you

Time

Time is relative,
don't take it personally

Self

Knowing yourself in the moment is
the only way to understand others

Others

Without others,
there would be no you

Reclaim your space: Your screens might take you to far-away places, but they also lock you down in one particular spot. What uncharted areas of your home might have been neglected in favor of the couch/TV vortex? What are some other possibilities for them? Here's what I discovered...

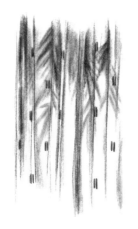

I used to watch TV while I ate
breakfast. I switched to eating
at the dining table and now I
watch the wind blow branches
every morning, casting long,
leafy silhouettes on my curtains
like a projector on a movie screen.

Instead of putting a TV in
our bedroom, I arranged a large
mirror on the dresser to open up
the space. A screen-free room
helps me fall asleep faster.

I moved our comfy armchair
to the closest window with the
brightest light. I use it as my
reading chair when I need a
break from screens.

The couch/TV vortex always pulled me away from my dining table - now, if I'm not eating on it, I use it for projects.

Bathroom

Closet

Dining Room

Closet

Hallway

Bedroom

My bedroom is a rest-only space: Gentle lighting, heavy drapes, and tidy nightstands.

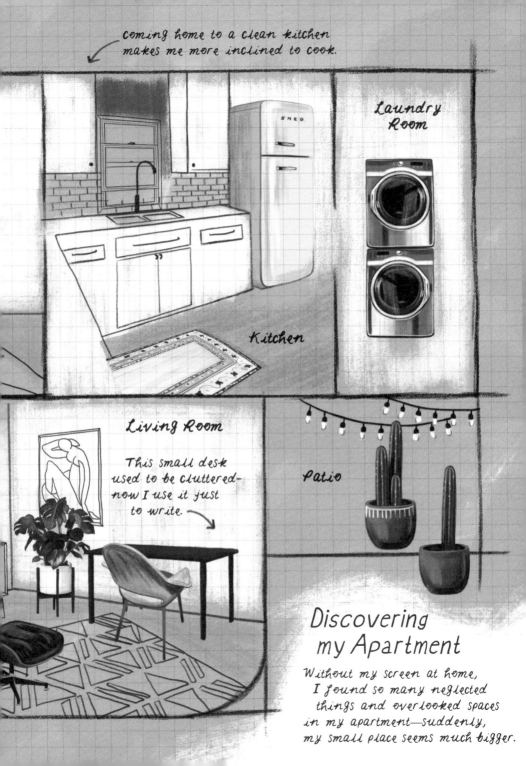

Map your space: Draw what surrounds you or rearrange reality. Think about how your space can transform once you change the focus.

What do you reach for?

When I need inspiration, or a brief break,
I look through the books I keep nearby.

Nearby Inspiration

A Break in Time

Set an alarm clock to remind you to take an hourly break from work. This will help you manage your time, without the distractions that come with a phone. Soon your internal clock will kick in and you won't need a physical one.

Meaningful Pauses: No matter what you do, taking brief offline pauses add up to a more fulfilling day.

- Take a ten-minute mindful walk: keeping your gaze averted, focus on your breath, be conscious of your feet each time they touch the ground and each time they lift off.

- Care for your eyes: focus on something in the distance. Then, very slowly, let your gaze find objects nearer and nearer to you, in the same line of sight.

- Draft a letter to a far-away friend, or write a poem, or make a sketch. Don't worry about it being perfect—focus on one important idea you've been thinking about.

- Brew some tea. Use loose leaf, and make it a quiet ritual you can look forward to. Spend time on the details of each step.

Task Landscape:
It can feel like we are organized by our to-do lists, rather than the other way around. Traditional lists emphasize quantity over quality, without regard to time spent, or true priorities. Simply because something took a lot of time, doesn't mean it's the most meaningful. Organize your tasks for the day as a landscape.

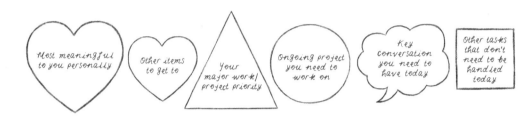

Here is my schedule:

Live like a Cat

Cats sleep approximately fourteen
hours a day, but when they're
awake they are hyper aware.
Use your awake hours wisely.
Give yourself time to focus,
reflect, rest, and play.

Exercise your emotions: Allowing yourself to feel uncomfortable emotions can help make difficult times a little easier. Don't ignore them! If you can't quite put words to what you are feeling, try exploring it through colors and textures.

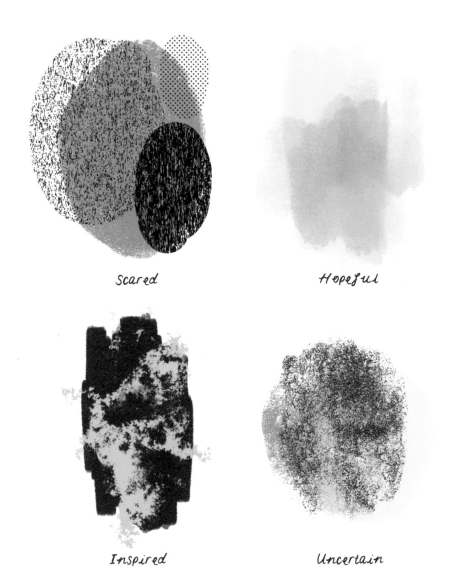

Scared

Hopeful

Inspired

Uncertain

Understand Yourself: You can learn a lot about yourself by creating a self-portrait. Here are some unique ways to depict yourself without taking a photograph.

1. Look at yourself in the mirror. Draw what you see in one continuous line without ever lifting your pencil from the page.

2. Paint yourself non-figuratively. Don't focus on making things "real;" instead, think of what you represent in that moment.

3. Draw a circle: inside of it, write down your dreams, loves, fears, and priorities until you have filled the entire space.

John Steinbeck said, "You can only understand people if you feel them in yourself." Think of three people in your life who you don't get along with and try to imagine what they are going through. Did you ever feel the same way?

ry to imagine

Traveling can be one of the best ways to disconnect
and gain perspective on a life cluttered with
distractions. These are places that I hope to visit
and learn from one day.

India

England

Nova Scotia

L.M. MONTGOMERY

Anne of Green

Hawaii

Morocco

Japan

Iceland

Egypt

Where Will you Go?

Stop and think about the places you would like to visit. Begin with the closest to you and map your journey outwards. Think about what you would like to see and who you hope to meet.

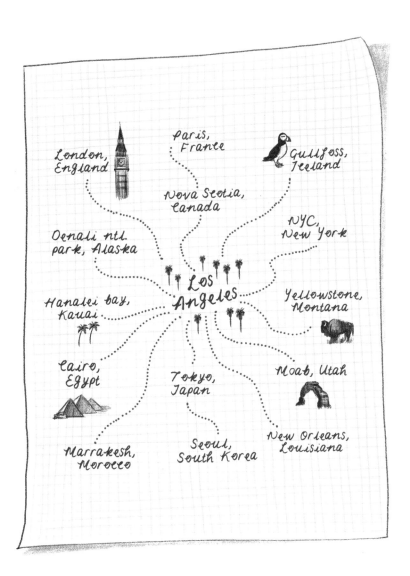

London, England

Paris, France

Gullfoss, Iceland

Nova Scotia, Canada

Denali ntl. park, Alaska

NYC, New York

Los Angeles

Hanalei bay, Kauai

Yellowstone, Montana

Cairo, Egypt

Tokyo, Japan

Moab, Utah

Marrakesh, Morocco

Seoul, South Korea

New Orleans, Louisiana

Offline Evening:
Rest & Reflection

"It's enough for me to be sure that you and I exist at this moment."
-Gabriel García Márquez

Unwind Offline:

Reflect on a day spent screen-free: How do you feel? Did you accomplish more than you expected? Did you notice something new or surprising? Now it's time to rest without distractions.

evening inventory

Rest: Appreciate everything you've accomplished today, and prepare for tomorrow.

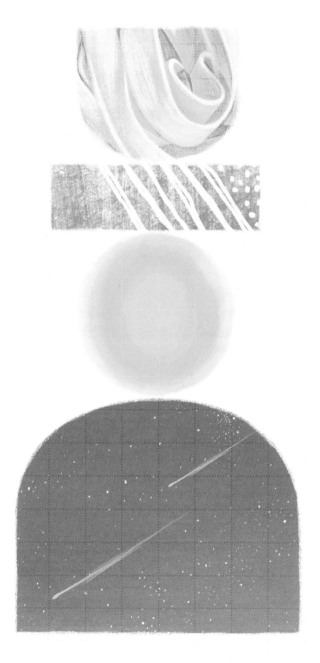

Rituals
Steps you practice everyday

Nourishment
What gives you energy
for tomorrow

Visualizing
Laying out your
thoughts and plans

True Rest
Shutting off your
mind so it can repair

B-Sides: Come home each evening looking forward to something that will enrich you. Create rituals like playing an album start to finish while you make dinner. The journey you take with the record will be 100% more meaningful than anything on a Spotify playlist.

Make a list of some of your favorite albums,
then write down the memory each one brings up.

Cooking seasonally is an easy,
everyday way to connect directly
with the earth, and the world
around you. Pasta is a great way to
experiment with seasonal produce
and different flavor combinations.
Go to the market, see what looks
fresh, and invent a dish.

Setting the Table:
We often eat our meals on coffee tables or our laps and use the couch as the dining room. Setting the table is an easy and healthy habit that lets you enjoy your dinner, and focus on either your dinner mate or yourself.

Break out the fancy china- even if it's just for you

Use a freshly picked bouquet as your centerpiece

Mix and match cloth napkins for fun.

What does your table look like?

Twilight Activity:

We often revert to watching TV at night because "there's nothing else to do." In fact, almost anything else is better! You will go to sleep happier, and feel more in touch with yourself.

Working on a puzzle is an activity that spans multiple evenings, especially if you have pets that can't stop walking on it.

If you have a little outdoor space, then having a firepit is a great way to get out in the evening, whether to sit around and talk, or have a reflective moment looking into the flames.

I always get excited whenever I open the mailbox and see something else besides bills. Sitting down and taking the time to write someone might just make their day (and yours).

Organizing might seem like the last thing you want to do when you get home, but getting it out of the way on a weeknight makes for full days off later, and more satisfaction at bedtime.

Something that I learned from my grandma is to enjoy a cup of tea before bed. There are plenty of blends that will help you sleep, curtail anxiety, and allow you to relax. The act of making tea can also be a soothing ritual in the evenings.

Prioritize your Time: Writing down your to-do's makes them less intimidating and also invites you to think of larger plans and life-goals. One small step is to ask: What can I do tonight to make tomorrow easier?

Brew coffee the night before for easy mornings

Prep some meals
for the week

Warm and Cool

Studies show that exposure to the blue glow of your phone or tablet at night can disrupt your sleep schedule. Surrounding yourself with warm light feels more natural and can help your room feel more cozy.

Louise Erdrich said, "When every inch of the world is known, sleep may be the only wilderness that we have left." Sleep is a crucially important part of life that we often fail to prioritize. Make sure to check in with yourself in the moments before you go to bed, and unplug from everything else.

How are you, right now?

Dream Journal: I keep a pen and paper on my bedside table so I can record my dreams as soon as I wake up. Sometimes dreams seem like movies, and it's easier to explain them to people through frames rather than writing. An exercise I like to do is draw them out into short comics.

What do you dream?

Look up at the stars and not down at your feet. Try to make sense of what you see, and wonder about what makes the universe exist. Be curious.
—Stephen Hawking